HAVE YOU PRAYED FOR YOUR PASTOR LATELY?

HAVE YOU PRAYED FOR YOUR PASTOR LATELY?

Deborah L. Grant

Published by: Unlock Publishing House
6715 Suitland Road
Morningside, Maryland 20746
www.unlockpublishinghouse.com
ISBN: 978-1-7327503-0-2

Printed in the United States of America August 2018

This book is dedicated to my brother Darris L. Bryson. I love you, and remember... It's not over until you win!!!

Acknowledgments

First, giving all glory and praise to my Lord and Savior Jesus Christ for all He has done and is doing in my life. It is an honor to be called a friend of God!

To my husband and best friend, Donald of 24 years. Thank you for your support and encouragement to go after whatever I want with passion and courage. Our future is bright! I love you!

To my three wonderful children, Jada, Donovan, and Nia. You are the wind beneath my wings. I love being your mother! You all are the best!!!

To my mom whom I call "Nanny." Thank you for introducing me to Christ at a young age and for teaching me how to pray about everything and give up in nothing. I love you and appreciate you!

To the best pastors in the world, Drs. Mike and DeeDee Freeman. Words will always be inadequate to express my appreciation for the many impartations I have received from your lives. I wish God could duplicate you and place you all over the world. The world needs what you are! I will always be a part of you, and I shall always represent the kingdom of God well. I cherish you both!

To my confidants, the Pastoral Staff of Spirit of Faith Christian Center. Your love and friendship are invaluable.

To the Intercessory team. Each one of you are jewels! Keep on praying; you are making great impact in the lives of many!

And last but not least, to Aiisha Davis. Thank you for all your hard work and dedication in helping me to complete this book. You are a treasure!

TABLE OF CONTENTS

Forward

Have You Prayed for Your Pastor Lately is both timely and necessary for the hour that we are living. Too many men and women of God are falling prey to the devices of the enemy. It is crucial that there are people who will commit to praying for or on behalf of their leaders. By comprising a book of prayers that she, herself, prays on behalf of Dr. Freeman, myself and the ministry, Minister Deborah has removed the struggle out of trying to figure out what to pray for your pastors.

Minister Deborah is an anointed woman of God that has the heart to pray for God's people. She has been the leader of our prayer ministry for many years. She is fully qualified to write such a book.

Our ministry was built on prayer, and it is because faithful partners have continued to join their faith with ours in prayer that our ministry is experiencing the tremendous success that it is today.

May you generously reap as you sow into your pastors' lives through your prayers.

Dr. DeeDee Freeman
Spirit of Faith Christian Center

How to Utilize This Book

This book was put together to serve as a springboard to your prayer life, to assist you in praying directly and specifically for your pastor. Every written prayer has been taken from the Word of God. There are many examples of this in scripture, such as Philippians 1:11, Ephesians 1:16-23, and Colossians 1:9-15.

As you read the prayer in this book, out loud unto the Father, believe you receive them done by faith. Mark 11:22 says, *"When you pray, believe you receive, and you shall have it."* You must know that God obligates Himself to His Word. He said Isaiah 55:11 [amp], *"So shall My Word be that goeth forth out of My mouth it shall not return unto me void, (empty, without producing any effect), but it shall accomplish what I please and prosper in the thing, for which it was sent."* Prayer is powerful when we believe by faith and receive what we are saying.

Now prayers of intercession are different; or should I say have different guidelines from the prayers of petition. When you are interceding on someone else's behalf, they have a vital part in the manifestation of those prayers coming to pass.

What our prayers do for the individual causes them to hear the voice of God concerning those areas for which we have prayed. Our prayers release angels to go to work on their behalf. It causes laborers to come along their path to share on the things we've prayed. There will be different encounters of many sorts to assist them in making wise decisions. The enemy will be exposed in different areas that he once hid. Ultimately, however, the individual must obey God and make decisions on their own volition.

Our prayers of intercession support and assist them in fulfilling God's desire and plan for their lives coming to fruition. I love being a part of that! You can take this book and make it a part of your prayer team's arsenal. You will be an instrument of change and increase for your church. I believe every person who partners with a local church or ministry should have this book in their possession. When you fervently pray for your shepherd, you will set yourself to receive from him/her live never before. It's difficult to be at odds with someone you're consistently praying for. A congregation of unified, Spirit-filled people is the Devils' biggest nightmare. Let's give him a real bad awakening!

Let's persistently pray for our pastors!

Introduction

I pray this book will announce to your spirit that you are vitally important and necessary in assisting your pastor to fulfill the mandate from God for his/her life and assignment. It is my desire that you will begin to avail yourselves to pray for your pastor daily with fervency and consistency. The word of God says in 2 Chronicles 16:9, *"that the eyes of the Lord are going to and fro in the earth looking for someone to show Himself strong on the behalf of."*

It is the order of God to use a man or woman of God to lead another man to the next level of life. He demonstrated this in the lives of Paul, Timothy, Elijah, Elisha, and many others. Your pastor stands on the front line of the battlefield, and he is the covering of the sheep. He intercedes on behalf of the people daily that we would experience the fullness of the promises of God and walk in our predestined purpose. Well, if he's covering us in prayer, we should be covering and upholding his arms in prayer. The Word of God speaks of this in Exodus 17:11-12, when Moses said to Joshua go out and fight with Amalek and tomorrow, I will stand on the top of the hill with the rod of God in my hand. When Moses' arms grew heavy, Aaron and Hur would hold his arms one on each side. As long as his hands were lifted, Israel prevails; but when his hands grew tired, Amalek would prevail against them. His hands being raised with the rod in it; symbolized his authority, leadership, and assignment from God.

Too many pastors are growing weary and overwhelmed with the assignments connected with the ministry and unfortunately dying before their time. We must preserve the lives of our pastors by assisting them in this regard. God needs leaders who are sensitive to His voice and bold and courageous enough to skillfully equip His people.

Are you ready to make an impact? The Word says in Ephesians 6:8, *"Whatsoever good any man doeth the same shall he receive of the Father."*

With that being said,

LET'S BEGIN!!!

The Purpose of a Pastor

My objective is to define and explain the role and purpose of the Pastor's gift to the body of Christ. Ephesians 4:11 -12 GNT says, "that he gave gifts to people...He did this to prepare all God's people for the work of Christian service, in order to build up the body of Christ."

Let's define Pastor because the power to define is the power to fulfill.

A true Pastor is a man or woman who is after the heart of God. He or She is a type of Shepherd. He or She cares for, feeds, protects and nurtures the sheep. 1Peter 5:2 – 3. AMP. "...a man [woman] after mine own [God's] heart...." Acts 13:22.

He or She loves, leads and lifts the people to become like Christ in their behavior, thinking, and living. Their lessons and instructions should stretch you beyond your normal limits, mindsets, inhibitions, and fears. Their teachings and actions expand other's capacity to believe God for more according to the principles found in God's word.

This man or woman has identified himself as an integral "PIECE" of the puzzle in assisting others to achieve their utmost purpose and potential in Christ! He or She continues to demonstrate by precept and example how to live a godly and prosperous life through. This is a result of obeying and practicing the word of God. He or She uses their life as a pattern to follow.

Here are some frequently asked questions, and the corresponding answers about the Pastor's role and office.

1. Why do I need a Pastor?

Their responsibility is to equip the saints to do the work of the ministry and to edifying the body. Also, for the unity of the faith and knowledge of Jesus, in order for saints to become mature and no longer children confused with a lot of misinformation. To release or awaken in the people their potential that they possess to effectively supply the body. To help you navigate your way to achieving your full potential in Christ on earth and to serve as a compass to help guide you. As you use a compass or map first to locate where you are, then it shows you where to go.

2. Can I simply choose any Pastor that I personally like?

Your pastor/ leader should be a person of upstanding integrity and moral character. Hebrews 6:12 says to "follow those who through faith and patience have inherited the promises". Your Pastor should have fruit of a righteous lifestyle and evidence of the things they teach and preach in their lives.

1 Corinthians 11:1 says "follow me as I follow Christ." Psalms 78:72 says, David lead them by his integrity of heart and by the skillfulness or proven experience. Hebrews 13:7 says, "…whose faith follow, considering the end or outcome of their conduct."

3. How will I know that I have identified the right one?

Matthew 11:29, 30 When this person ministers it challenges you, to dig in and become better in every area of your life. You can undoubtedly receive and understand how to apply what you've heard. Genesis 26:4, 5 This voice continues to speak to you when you're away from the person. WWPD (What Would Pastor Do) in this situation comes to mind. How would he or she obey the principles of God's words in this situation?

Their example of righteousness and integrity inspires you. You have been significantly challenged and changed as a result of hearing and doing the instructions from the word of God that they teach and live!

4. What was Gods purpose for giving us the gift of a Pastor ?

Ephesians 4:8 GNT "He gave gifts to his people." A Pastor is a gift given to help develop and lead people to fulfill their God-ordained destiny. It is the order of God to place a man or woman in another person's life to lead and guide them to the next level of life. We see this example in the lives of Paul and Timothy, Ruth and Naomi, and several others in the bible.

Now that we have God's perspective on the purpose of the gift of the Pastor, lets [let's] fervently pray on their behalf.

Prayer for Pastor

Father, I bless and adore You. You are the Great Shepherd. Your Word declares that You will leave the ninety-nine who are found and go after the one who is lost. Thank You for being the keeper of our souls. I give You praise for the gift you've given the Bod of Christ through the office of the pastor.

May Your intended purpose and desire be fulfilled through pastor's life and ministry to cause Your people to mature spiritually, to be edified and to come into the unity of the faith. Your Word declares that You will give Your people pastors who are after Your heart, that will feed them with knowledge and understanding concerning Your Word, and that You will give them wisdom to lead and guide Your people into green pastures.

May Pastor ____________ always be a willing and obedient vessel of honor, meat for Your use. I pray that the congregation of *(Name of Church)* will always esteem and respect his/her God-given position and authority. I come against and bind the spirit of opposition and every hindrance concerning pastor's assignment, marriage, family, finances, and vision. Satan, you are already a defeated foe. I speak confusion to every plot you have devised and set up against his/her life, now in Jesus' Name. I declare that Your power and Your agape love flow mightily through my Pastor's life to bless and empower Your people like never before.

In Jesus Name, Amen

Ephesians 4:11-13, "And He Himself gave some to be apostles, some prophets, some evangelists, and some pastors and teachers, for the equipping of the saints for the work of ministry, for the edifying of the body of Christ, till we all come to the unity of the faith and of the knowledge of the Son of God, to a perfect man, to the measure of the stature of the fullness of Christ."

Jeremiah 3:15, "And I will give you shepherds according to My heart, who will feed you with knowledge and understanding. "

1 Peter 5:2-4, "Shepherd the flock of God which is among you, serving as overseers, not by compulsion but willingly, not for dishonest gain but eagerly; not being lords over those entrusted to you but being examples to the flock."

Prayer for Pastor's Marriage

Father, I extol Your name. You are the covenant-keeping God. Marriage is a covenant that You have established to show the world Your preparing bride. I lift up my pastor's marriage unto You. I pray that my pastor loves his/her spouse purely and sincerely with not only Eros love but Agape love.

I pray that they will take some time away from ministry to spend quality time with each other. May they always be each other's closest friend and confidant. I bind the spirit of division, in Jesus name and I loose unity and peace. Your Word declares that where unity is, there is the commanded blessing.

I thank You, Father, that they will always live their lives as an open book. Your Word declares that we are to be living epistles to be read by men. May integrity always guide their every decision and action. I pray that they will keep You first and each other as their next priority and responsibility.

I pray that they always walk in forgiveness forbearing one another in love, not rendering evil for evil. I pray that they will always have mutual respect and adoration for each other, always having one another's back as a true relationship should. I thank You that You that You will lift their relationship as a trophy in Your hand, to demonstrate to the world Your intended plan and purpose for marriage from the beginning. Bless them with many years of happiness, prosperity, and abundant joy.

In Jesus Name, Amen

---

1 Peter 3:7, "Husbands, likewise, dwell with them with understanding, giving honor to the wife, as to the weaker vessel, and as being heirs together of the grace of life, that your prayers may not be hindered."

Ephesians 5:21, "Be subject to one another out of reverence for Christ (the Messiah, the Anointed One)."

Colossians 3:18-19, "Wives, submit to your own husbands, as is fitting in the Lord. Husbands love your wives and do not be bitter toward them.

Prayer for Pastor's Children

Father in the name of Jesus, I lift up pastor's children to You. I lift up my pastor's children to You. Your Word declares that children are a heritage unto You and the fruit of the womb is Your reward. May Pastor _________________ children always keep You first in their lives, living holy and pure before You. May they succeed academically and prosper in every area of their lives.

Let wisdom govern their decision-making even as it comes to the selection of their friends and also whom they will marry. I decree that no weapon that is formed against them will prosper and every tongue that is formed against them they will condemn. As Godly character develops in their lives, I pray that they have boldness in sharing their faith and personal testimonies wherever they go.

Raise them up as trophies in Your hand to demonstrate to the world Your intended purpose for Godly seed in the earth. I decree that the generation of the upright is blessed, and the seed of the righteous shall be delivered!

In Jesus Name, Amen

Ephesians 6:1-3, "Children, obey your parents in the Lord, for this is right. Honor your father and mother, which is the first commandment with promise: that it may be well with you and you may live long on the Earth."

Psalms 112:2, "His descendants will be mighty on Earth; the generation of the upright will be blessed."

Proverbs 6:20-22, "My son, keep your father's command. And do not forsake the law of your mother. Bind them continually upon your heart; time them around your neck. When you roam, they will lead you; when you sleep, they will keep you, and when you awake, they will speak with you."

Prayer for Divine Health

Father, I praise You and adore You, for You are Jehovah Rapha, the Lord who is our healer. Your Word declares that by the stripes of Jesus, we are already healed. I lift up my pastor unto You declaring that he/she walks in the finished work that took place at Calvary. Jesus was wounded for our transgression, bruised for our iniquities, the chastisement of our peace was upon Him, and with His stripes, and we are now the healed of God. I forbid sickness and disease from operating in Pastor's ________________ body.

I render every attack powerless now, in Jesus name. I bind the spirit of infirmity, and I uproot every generational curse from continuing in Jesus name. Satan, the blood of Jesus is against you. I command every organ, every cell, every tissue, blood vessel, nerve, and joint to function in the original perfection that is was created to function in from the beginning.

I declare that the anointing is destroying every yoke and removing every burden of stress, anxiety, and sickness now, in Jesus name. I trouble now what has been troubling my pastor, in Jesus name. Father, I thank You for wholeness.

Your shalom be upon Pastor's body causing nothing to be missing, or nothing is broken in his/her life. Now I release Your peace to come upon him/her like a river and guard his/her heart and mind through our Lord Jesus Christ. I pray that he/she will believe the report of the Lord and rejoice in the God of his/her salvation, Jehovah Rapha; You are his/her healer.

In Jesus Name, Amen

---

3 John 1:2 [amp], "Beloved, I pray that you may prosper in every way and [that your body] may keep well, even as [I know] your soul keeps well and prospers."

Psalms 103:1-5, "Bless the Lord, O my soul and all that is within me, bless His holy name! Bless the Lord, o my soul and forget not all His benefits who forgives all your iniquities, who heals all your diseases, who redeems your life from destruction, who crowns you with lovingkindness and tender mercies, who satisfies your mouth with good things, so that your youth is renewed like the eagle's."

Prayer for Personal Prosperity

Father, I give You glory. For You are El Shaddai, the God of More than Enough. Your Word declares that You are able to do exceedingly, abundantly, above all things that we could ever ask or think according to the power that is at work on the inside of us. I thank You, that as Your children we have a legacy of wealth because of the covenant You made with Abraham.

I lift up Pastor ________________ unto You. I thank You that he/she indeed has a revelation of true Bible prosperity, that he/she is prosperous spiritually, financially, emotionally and relationally. Your Word says You wish above all things that we prosper and be in health even as our souls prosper.

I pray that You would give Pastor wisdom to make wise investments and decisions. Remove every hidden trap and snare of the enemy and causes Satan's every plot to be revealed and rejected by our pastor.

Your Word declares that we are blessed to be a blessing, so with this empowerment that You have given him/her, I pray that he/she reproduces men and women who will also walk in true biblical prosperity where there is nothing missing and nothing broken in their lives.

As Pastor stands as a vessel of honor reaping the rewards of righteousness and a diligent lifestyle, may he/she also continue to stand regardless of the persecution that shall arise. Allow him/her to be confident concerning the manifestations that will come as a result of the blessing that is upon his/her life

In Jesus Name, Amen

Psalms 1:1-3, "Blessed is the man who walks not in the counsel of the ungodly, nor stands in the path of sinners, nor sits in the seat of the scornful; but his delight is in the law of the Lord, and in His law he meditates day and night. He shall be like a tree planted by the rivers of water that brings forth its fruit in its season, whose leaf also shall not wither; and whatever he does shall prosper."

3 John 2:1, "Beloved, I pray that you may prosper in all things and be in health, just as your soul prospers."

Prayer for Pastors Heart

Father, in Jesus name I pray that my pastor guards his/her heart with all diligence. For out of it flows the issues of life. May Pastor ________________ always keep a pure heart toward You and Your people. I pray that the everyday contaminates of the world will not enter in and choke the Word and cause it to be unfruitful.

May Pastors always be quick to forgive and to pray on others' behalf. Your Word declares that You will keep him in perfect peace, whose mind is stayed on You.

I thank You for creating in him/her a clean heart and renewing the right spirit within him/her. Allow Your agape love to motivate and inspire every word that is spoken out of his/her mouth and every action he/she will ever take.

Protect Pastor from people who do not have his/her best interest at heart Allow him/her to see You in his/her life like never before because he/she possesses a pure heart.

In Jesus Name, Amen

Proverbs 4:23, "Keep your heart with all diligence, for out of it spring the issues of life."

Psalms 24:3-5, "Who may ascend into the hill of the Lord? Or who may stand in His holy place He who has clean hands and a pure heart who has not lifted up his soul to an idol, nor sworn deceitfully. He shall receive blessings from the Lord, and righteousness from the God of his salvation."

Prayer for Friendships

Father, I pray that You would surround my Pastor with good friends; people with whom he/she can connect and have fellowship with. May people of like precious faith be drawn to him/her because of the agape love he/she displays. Your Word says, *"He that hath friends must show himself friendly."*

I declare that Pastor ___________________ friends have an understanding of the value of true covenant relationships and the responsibility that comes with them. Allow the time spent with his/her friends to be times of fun as well as the time of iron sharpening iron.

I come against the spirit of division and forbid it from destroying any key relationships that You have ordained. Father, I thank You that Pastor is aware of anyone who does not have his/her best interest at heart and he/she is able to discern, forgive, and move on in the spirit of love.

Thank You Lord that my pastor has wonderful friendships that glorify You and enhance his/her life and ministry.

In Jesus Name, Amen

Proverbs 18:24, "A man who has friends must himself be friendly, but there is a friend who sticks closer than a brother."

John 15:13, "Greater love has no one than one this, than to lay down one's life for his friends."

Job 42:10, "And the Lord restored Job's losses when he prayed for his friends. Indeed the Lord gave Job twice as much as he had before."

Prayer for Protection

Father, I pray for my pastor's safety and protection. I declare Your promise found in Isaiah 54:17 that says, *"No weapon formed against you shall prosper, and every tongue which rises against you in judgment You shall condemn."*

Father, I ask You that You shield and protect my pastor from people who do not have his/her best interest at heart. Bring to light every hidden agenda that will cause harm to my pastor. Give unto him/her a discerning spirit to know and recognize improper motives and intentions.

Thank You Lord that Pastor ___________________ is kept secure by the Word of Your power. Satan, I bind you now. Every plot and scheme that you have devised against my pastor, I speak confusion to that strategy now, in Jesus name.

I declare that 1,000 may fall at on side, and 10,000 at his/her right hand, but it shall not come near his/her dwelling. He/she will fulfill his/her God-given assignment on time unhindered and unchecked by any demonic force or opposition.

Thank You Father that my pastor dwells in safety all the days of his/her life.

In Jesus Name, Amen

Isaiah 54:17, "No weapon formed against you shall prosper, and every tongue which rises against you in judgment you shall condemn. This is the heritage of the servants of the Lord and their righteousness is from Me, says the Lord."

Luke 10:19, "Behold! I have given you authority and power to trample upon serpents and scorpions, and [physical and mental strength and ability] over all the power that the enemy [possesses]; and nothing shall in any way harm you."

Prayer for Perception and Discernment

Father, in the name of Jesus, I pray that my pastor has 20/20 vision concerning spiritual matters and is able to discern the times and season we are in as a ministry.

May the eyes of his/her understanding be enlightened to become keenly aware of the things he/she needs to know that is necessary to fulfill the vision which You have given him/her.

May Pastor _______________ never be caught off guard or be taken advantage of by any plot or scheme of the enemy. Your Word says, *"My sheep know My voice and the voice of a stranger they will not follow."*

Holy Spirit, I thank You for leading my pastor in truth and showing him/her things that are to come.

I decree that Pastor is used as an instrument of precision and is on point for every assignment and goal. Even as he/she ministers, may he/she always have an accurate spoken word, in due season for Your people.

Thank You for giving him/her insight, foresight, and oversight to care for Your people in order that each partner will be thoroughly equipped and furnished for every good work.

In Jesus Name, Amen

Ephesians 1:17-21, "That the God of our Lord Jesus Christ, the Father of glory, may give to you the spirit of wisdom and revelation in the knowledge of Him, the eyes of yourunderstanding being enlightened; that you may know what is the hope of His calling, what are the riches of the glory of His inheritance in the saints, and what is the exceeding greatness of His power toward us who believe, according to the workingof His mighty power which He worked in Christ when He raised Him from the dead and seated Him at His right hand in the heavenly places, far above all principality and power and might and dominion, and every name that is named, not only in this age but also in that which is to come."

2 Corinthians 4:18, "While we do not look at the things which are seen, but at the things which are not seen. For the things, which are seen are temporary, but the things, which are not seen, are eternal."

Prayer for Integrity

Father, in the name of Jesus, I praise You for a pastor who walks in integrity and righteousness. Your Word says that, *"The integrity of the upright would guide them."*

I declare that my pastor has a good name because Your word says, *"Having a good name is rather to be chosen than fine riches."*

I declare that Pastor ________________ resist the temptations of the flesh to compromise morals and standards of righteousness in any area. Cause him/her to recognize sin afar off and give no place to the devil, but to always remain submitted unto You, in Jesus name.

I pray that Pastor leads the ministry by example and is living proof and bears the fruit in his/her life of one whom You will honor and satisfy with good things because he/she walks uprightly before You.

I bind every evil and seducing spirit form alluring Pastor ______________ to get him/her off course. I pray that he/she will never follow the voice of a stranger.

I declare that because of his/her relationship with you, sin will never be tolerated in his/her life. I thank you that Pastor leads his/her life as a living epistle to be read of all men.

In Jesus Name, Amen

Proverbs 20:7 [amp], "The righteous man walks in his integrity; blessed (happy, fortunate, enviable) are his children after him."

Psalms 78:72 [amp], "So [David] was their shepherd with an upright heart; he guided them by the discernment and skillfulness [which controlled] his hands."

Prayer for the Vision

Father, Your Word says, *"Write the vision and make it plan so that they may run that readeth it."* I thank You for giving the vision for (Your Church Name) to Pastor _______________. Send partners who will come from the North, South, East, and West to support the vision with their prayers, their time, their talent, and their treasures.

Let the partners have a heart and mind to work. I pray that the vision is thoroughly provided for and supported. I thank You that everything we need to grow and expand is already released to us. I release Your mighty hand to be seen in the earth realm like never before.

Cause the heathens that are around and about us to know that You have built this vision, and cause desolated places to be inhabited and transformed like the garden of Eden.

May this vision go forth unhindered by any satanic force or opposition. Satan, every plan and purpose you have devised to prevent the vision from prospering, and succeeding is bound now, in Jesus Name.

Thank You for the vision of *(Your Church Name)*. May it prosper and do Your Kingdom good as it erects as a monument of hope, life, and change for Your glory.

In Jesus Name, Amen

Habakkuk 2:2,3, "Then the Lord answered me and said: Write the vision and make it plain on tablets, that he may run who reads it. For the vision is yet for an appointed time, but at the end it will speak, and it will not lie. Though it tarries, wait for it; because it will surely come, it will not tarry."

Proverbs 29:18, "Where there is no revelation, the people cast off restraint; but happy is he who keeps the law."

Prayer for Personal Growth

Father, I thank you that my pastor is always persistent and in hot pursuit of more of Your presence, to know You more and more each day. Even as the deer pants for the water, I pray that my pastor longs after You.

May he/she have a desire to seek knowledge, and as he/she seeks more knowledge, give him/her not only information but also revelation of Your word like never before.

I thank You, that Pastor __________________ will never become satisfied with his/her present level of success and achievement but rather use it as a stepping stone to go into his/her next level and next wealthy place.

Your Word says, *"Let not the wise man glory in his wisdom, neither let the rich man glory in his riches, but let him that glories glory in this; that he knows and understands Me."* I decree that scripture in my pastor's life now and forevermore.

Thank You Father that my pastor is always being promoted and entrusted with more because of the faithfulness he/she has demonstrated at the present level.

I declare that he/she is consistently growing in new levels of faith, power, and authority.

In Jesus Name, Amen

Jeremiah 9:224 [amp], "But let him who glories glory in this: that he understands and know Me [personally and practically, directly discerning and recognizing My character], that I am the Lord, Who practices loving-kindness, judgment, and righteousness in the earth, for in these things I delight, says the Lord."

Philippians 3:10 [amp], "[For my determined purpose is] that I may know Him [that I may progressively become more deeply and intimately acquainted with Him, perceiving and recognizing and understanding the wonders of His Person more strongly and more clearly], and that I may in that same way come to know the power outflowing from His resurrection [which it exerts over believers], and that I may so share His sufferings as to be continually transformed [in spirit into His likeness even] to His death, [in the hope]."

Prayer for the Anointing

Father, in the name of Jesus, I thank You for the anointing upon Pastor ________________ life. May that anointing causes many burdens to be removed and yokes to be destroyed in the lives of Your people. Allow people to be drawn to You because of the manifestation of Your power that is present in our services.

As Pastor opens his/her mouth to minister Your Word, let it be as in the days of Solomon, how when he had finished speaking, Your glory filled the house, and the people poured their hearts in worship unto You like never before.

I release the same anointing to give Pastor strategies and wisdom for every endeavor that he/she seeks to fulfill and accomplish. Cause Your people to know that You are God and You will deliver them with Your mighty hand today, just as in times past.

I thank You that the anointing will cause the sick to recover, the lame to walk, the blind to see, the oppressed to be healed and restores an the broken-hearted to be mended.

Thank You Father, for a man/woman of God [illegible] full of the anointing of Holy Spirit, which will cause change to happen in the lives of Your people like never before.

In Jesus Name, Amen

Isaiah 10:27, "It shall come to pass in that day that his burden will be taken away from your shoulder, and his yoke from your neck, and the yoke will be destroyed because of the anointing oil."

1 John 2:27, "But the anointing which you have received from Him abides in you, and you do not need that anyone teach you; but as the same anointing teaches you concerning all things, and is true, and is not a lie, and just as it has taught you, you will abide in Him."

Prayer for Provision

Father, I thank You for being Jehovah Jireh, our provider. I pray that my pastor walks in perpetual abundant prosperity. I declare that every spiritual, emotional, physical, and financial need is met now, in Jesus name.

I come against lack in any manner from being in his/her life, in Jesus Name. I decree that he/she will always have more than enough to meet every budget for this ministry as well as every personal goal for every good endeavor.

Your word says that, *"You are able to make all grace abound towards us that we have all sufficiency and all things and abound in every good work."* I decree that word in my pastor's life. May You always supply his/her every need according to Your abundant riches that are in Christ Jesus.

Because You are El Shaddai, (The God of More than Enough), I fully expect that there will always be an overflow of provision for each phase of this vision. I decree that it will come to pass and flourish on time without hindrance.

Let Your will be done and accomplished in excellence. Because You are a first-class God, I declare Pastor

_________________ will always go first –class in life, because as You are, so are we in this earth realm. Hallelujah!

In Jesus Name, Amen

Isaiah 54:17, "No weapon formed against you shall prosper, and every tongue which rises against you in judgment you shall condemn. This is the heritage of the servants of the Lord and their righteousness is from Me, Says the Lord."

Luke 10:19 [Amp], "Behold! I have given you authority and power to trample upon serpents and scorpions, and [physical and mental strength and ability] over all the power that the enemy [possesses]; and nothing shall in any way harm you."

Prayer for Joy

Father, I pray that my pastor has joy, unspeakable and full of glory. Your Word says that, *"The joy of the Lord is our strength."* So I decree that Pastor ________________ be strengthened with all might in his/her inner man.

When situations and circumstances seem to be overwhelming, may joy arise in his/her spirit and cause him/her to sing spiritual songs and hymns in adoration unto You, to cause burdens to be removed and yokes to be destroyed and every weight to be thrown off, in Jesus Name. I bind discouragement in Jesus name.

As Pastor casts all of his/her cares upon You, may he/ she continue to trust You with all of his/her heart, leaning not unto his/her own understanding, but always staying in the peace and the rest of God.

Thank You Father that the Joy of the Lord is Pastor's strength, and enablement to do great things for You and to live the abundant life daily.

In Jesus Name, Amen

Hebrews 13:17, "Obey those who rule over you, and be submissive, for they watch out for your souls, as those who must give account. Let them do so with joy and not with grief, for that would be unprofitable for you."

John 15:10, 11, "If you keep My commandments, you will abide in my love, just as I have kept My Father's commandments and abide in His love. These things I have spoken to you, that My joy may remain in you, and that your joy may be full."

Prayer for Travel and Itineraries

Father, in the name of Jesus, I lift up my pastor as he/she is on travel at this time. I thank You that Your angels are encamped about Pastor ___________________, to keep him/her in all of his/her ways. Thank You that they are there to defend, protect, and preserve his/her going out and his/her coming in.

Psalms 91 declares that, He who dwells in the secret place of the Most High shall abide under the shadow of the Almighty; therefore no evil shall befall him/her. For 1,000 will fall at his/her side, 10,000 at his/her right hand, but it shall not come nigh him/her.

I decree Your favor to go ahead of Pastor to cause him/her to be entreated as Your ambassador. Allow him/her to experience sweatless victories as well as have an enjoyable time as he/she is on Your assignment.

I take authority over every principality and every power assigned to the region to which he/she is going. I forbid you Satan from preventing or hindering the will of God form taking place in any way.

Holy Spirit, I release You to have Your way to do whatever is necessary through Pastor to cause Your people to be blessed. I give You praise for safe traveling grace and mercy.

In Jesus Name, Amen

Ephesians 6:19, "And [pray] also for me, that [freedom of] utterance may be given me, that I may open my mouth to proclaim boldly the mystery of the good news (the Gospel)."

Psalms 91:11, "For He shall give His angels charge over you to keep you in all of your ways."

Prayer for the Ministerial Staff

Father, I pray that the ministers of *(Name of Church)* have a heart after You and have embraced the heart of their pastor. May they always be divinely led by Your Spirit. For those who are led by Your Spirit are truly the sons of God.

May they give watchful care to the sheep, assisting the pastor in the vision You've given to him/her. Teach them how to be a good help, problem solvers, and innovative thinkers to help the ministry to thrive and generously meet the needs of Your people.

May the staff of *(Name of Church)* always be alert and sober-minded, knowing that the adversary seeks to bring division and strife among Godly leadership. May Your agape love flow out of each minister and may they always be motivated by love, and keep a pure heart to serve the pastor and Your people.

As they sow, may they also reap, and with the same measure that they give out, may it be measured back to them again.

Thank You Father that we have the best ministerial team, anointed and appointed by You to help build and edify this church under the leadership of Pastor ______________

In Jesus Name, Amen

---

2 Corinthians 6:3-4, "We give no offense in anything, that our ministry may not be blamed. But in all things we commend ourselves as ministers of God: in much patience, in tribulations, in needs, in distresses, in stripes, in imprisonments, in tumults, in labors, in sleeplessness, in fasting.

1 Corinthians 4:1-2, "Let a man so consider us, as servants of Christ and stewards of the mysteries of God. Moreover, it is required in stewards that one be found faithful."

2 Corinthians 3:5-6, "Not that we are sufficient of ourselves to think of anything as being from ourselves, but our sufficiency is from God, who also made us sufficient as ministers of the new covenant, not of the letter but of the Spirit; for the letter kills, but the Spirit gives life."

Prayer for the Congregation

Father, in the name of Jesus, I lift up the congregation at *(Name of Church)* that is under the leadership of Pastor ________________. May each partner be filled with the knowledge of Your will and all wisdom and spiritual understanding and walk worthy of the Lord unto all pleasing, being fruitful in every good work and increasing in the knowledge of God.

May the partners be strengthened with all might according to Your glorious power, unto all patience, and long-suffering, with joyfulness I decree that we are a church that is unified in the faith having the same mind and singleness of heart.

May the partners of *(Name of Church)* always uphold the arms of our pastor by praying for him/her daily and by taking ownership of the vision of this ministry, while serving in it as if it was their very own; giving thanks unto the Father, which has made us meet to be partakers of the inheritance of the saints in light.

May we continue in the faith, grounded and settled, and be not moved from the hope of the gospel, which we have heard. I declare that each partner walks in divine health and experiences increase and promotion in every area of their lives. As we set our affection to Your house, Your Word says, You will take care of our house.

I thank You that the congregation of *(Name of Church)* will assist Pastor ________________ in doing great things to impact this world.

In Jesus Name, Amen

Psalms 100:3, "Know that the Lord, He is God; it is He who has made us, and not we ourselves. We are His people and the sheep of His pasture."

John 10:27-29, "My sheep hear My voice, and I know them, and they follow Me. And I give them eternal life, and they shall never perish; neither shall anyone snatch them out of My hand. My Father, who has given them to Me, is greater than all; and no one is able to snatch them out of My Father's hand."

Psalms 79:13, "So We, Your people and sheep of Your pasture, Will give You thanks forever. We will show forth Your praise to all generations."

Prayer for Doors of Utterance

Father, in the name of Jesus, I lift up my pastor unto You. I thank You for giving him/her doors of utterance to make known the living Word of God.

Cause him/her to open his/her mouth boldly, without compromise to share Your powerful truth that will enable men to be strong and committed to Your work and the ministry of the Lord Jesus Christ.

Angels, I dispatch you now to go ahead of Pastor ____________________, to prepare the way for his/her arrival. I come against every satanic form of opposition now, in Jesus name.

And by Your Spirit, I take possession over the territory to which he/she is about to enter. I seize it now for Your plans and purposes to be established and accomplished.

Let Your Word flow richly, powerfully, and in demonstration so that the people there will be saved, healed, and delivered, in Jesus name.

Thank You for Your great favor encompassing Pastor as a shield. As he/she presents Your Word, may he/she be received as Your ambassador sent to do business on Your behalf. Use him/her for Your glory.

In Jesus Name, Amen

Ephesians 6:19 [Amp], "And [pray] also for me, that [freedom of] utterance may be given me, that I may open my mouth to proclaim boldly the mystery of the good news (the Gospel)."

Colossians 4:3-4, "Meanwhile praying also for s, that God would open to us a door for the word, to speak the mystery of Christ, for which I am also in chains, that may make it manifest, as I ought to speak."

Mark 16:15 [Amp], "And He said to them, Go into all the world and preach and publish openly the good news (the Gospel) to every creature [of the whole human race]."

Prayer for Prayer Life

Father, I pray that Pastor _________________ hunger and thirst for Your presence increases more and more. As the deer pants for the water may his/her soul continuously long after you.

May Pastor set aside quiet and intimate time to fellowship and commune with You daily, casting the whole of his/her care upon You because you care so affectionately for him/her. Your Word says, if we call upon You, that You will answer us and show us great and mighty things we do not know.

Thank You Father, for answering and giving direction and instructions, even comfort in challenging times unto my pastor. Just as Abraham was called Your friend, allow Pastor to draw closer to You just as one would their closest friend, entrusting every matter that concerns him/her into Your hands.

May Pastor's prayer life be effectual and fervent, always availing much, causing tremendous power to be made available to him/her and your people.

In Jesus Name, Amen

Acts 6:4, "But we will give ourselves continually to prayer and to the ministry of the word."

Philippians 4:6 [Amp], "Do not fret or have any anxiety about anything, but in every circumstance and in everything by prayer and petition (definite request), with thanksgiving, continue to make your wants known to God."

James 5:13, "Is anyone among you suffering? Let him pray. Is anyone cheerful? Let him sing Psalms.

Prayer for Ministry of the Word

Father, in Jesus name, I pray for my pastor as he/she ministers the Word. May the Word fall upon good ground and produce a bountiful harvest in the lives of the hearers. May it be fresh revelation knowledge to set at liberty those who are captive, remove every burden, and destroy every yoke of bondage.

Your Word is able to build us up and give us an inheritance. I declare that many will walk in their God-given purpose and receive their inheritance as a result of the Word Pastor ______________ delivers.

I bind every hindering spirit that would prevent the Word from going forth. I declare that there will not be any distractions to divert the attention of the people from receiving Your Word.

Give Pastor simplistic illustrations and examples to convey Your Word in such a way that even a child will be able to understand it.

Thank You Father, that this Word will cause deliverance and invoke an awesome change to take place in the lives of the people who will hear it.

I decree that their lives will never be the same!

In Jesus Name, Amen

Psalms 119:130 [Amp], "The entrance and unfolding of Your words give light; their unfolding gives understanding (discernment and comprehension) to the simple."

2 Timothy 4:2, "Preach the word! Be ready in season and out of season. Convince, rebuke, exhort, with all longsuffering and teaching."

Jeremiah 23:29, "Is not My word like a fire?" Says the Lord, "And like a hammer that breaks the rock in pieces?"

Prayer for Pastors Study Time

Father, I pray for my pastor as he/she studies Your Word. You said, *"Study to show ourselves approved unto You a workman that need not be ashamed, but rightly dividing the Word of truth."*

I call forth fresh revelation knowledge, wisdom, and understanding concerning Your divine truth into the heart of my pastor.

May Pastor ________________ have an inner witness to perceive a word in due season for this hour in order that yokes be destroyed and burdens be removed in the lives of the people that hear it.

Allow Pastor to have peaceable, quiet time to meditate and hear plainly from You. Give him/her illustration and examples to cause even a child to understand and be able to carry out Your Word.

I thank You that my pastor has an ear to hear what the Spirit of the Lord is saying to the church in this hour.

I decree that his/her study time is fruitful and beneficial and will cause increase and growth in his/her life personally and for the many that will hear the Word he/she ministers.

In Jesus Name, Amen

---

2 Timothy 2:15 [Amp], "Study and be eager and do your utmost to present yourself to God approved (tested by trial), a workman who has no cause to be ashamed, correctly analyzing and accurately dividing [rightly handling and skillfully teaching] the word of Truth."

Joshua 1:8, "This Book of the Law shall not depart from your mouth, but you shall meditate in it day and night that you may observe to do according to all that is written in it. For then you will make your way prosperous and then you will have good success."

Prayer for Building Projects

Father, I come in agreement with my pastor's heart concerning this part of the vision that You have given him/her to build. I pray that as we set our affection to build in Your house that this ministry will have an abundance of people who will give of their time, talent, treasure, and prayers to cause every aspect of this project to be supplied in abundance.

You said in Your Word, to enlarge the place of our tent and stretch forth the curtains of our habitations, to fear not, to lengthen our cords and strengthen our stakes.

I declare that we shall break forth on the right and on the left and that our seed shall inherit the earth and cause desolate cities to be inhabited, and possess the land. I decree that Your favor will go ahead of us and encompass us as a shield to cause *(Name of Church)* to have sweat less victory.

I decree every phase of this project be fully supplied in abundance to the glory and honor of Your name. And as we build it, send people from the North, South, East and West to come and be saved, healed, delivered and supportive of the vision You have given to Pastor ________________. I declare that we shall occupy until You come.

In Jesus Name, Amen

---

1 Chronicles 29:3, "Moreover, because I have set my affection on the house of my God, I have given to the house of my God, over and above all that I have prepared for the holy house, my own special treasure of gold and silver."

Isaiah 54:2, "Enlarge the place of your tent, and let them stretch out the curtains of your dwellings; do not spare; Lengthen your cords, and strengthen your stakes."

Ezekiel 36:34-36, "The desolate land shall be tilled instead of lying desolate in the sight of all who pass by. So they will say, 'This land that was desolate has become like the Garden of Eden; and the wasted, desolate, and ruined cities are now fortified and inhabited.' Then the nations, which are left all around you, shall know that I the Lord have rebuilt the ruined places and planted what was desolate. I, the Lord, have spoken it, and I will do it."

Prayer for Provision of the Ministry

Father, in the name of Jesus, I thank You that Pastor ____________________ knows You as his/her Jehovah Jireh. You are the God that sees ahead and makes all provision.

I declare that this ministry will never suffer lack of any kind. You said in Your Word that You are able to make all grace abound towards us, that we would have all sufficiency in all things and abound to every good work.

Thank You Father that You have given my pastor a good work to perform. I thank You Father that each and every endeavor that You've given him/her to fulfill will be fully supplied and nothing lacking in Jesus name.

I declare that every hindering spirit is bound now in Jesus name. I pray that the partners of *(Name of Church)* are obedient to Your Word concerning tithes and offerings. Your Word declares that as we set our affection towards Your house we will have our own proper good in our house.

Thank You Father, where You have given a vision there will always be a release of Your provision coupled with Your favor to get the job done. We receive it done now!

In Jesus Name, Amen

Philippians 4:19, "And my God shall supply all your needs according to His riches in glory by Christ Jesus."

II Corinthians 9:8, "And God is able to make all grace abound toward you, that you, always having all sufficiency in all things, may have an abundance for every good work."

Prayer for the Peace of God

Father, in the name of Jesus, I decree that my pastor remains in Your abundant peace. May Your peace that surpasses all understanding guard and keeps his heart and mind through our Lord and Savior Jesus Christ.

I pray that his home is a place where angels can reside and not feel out of place. I decree that my pastor will have a sweet sleep because of Your mighty uninterrupted peace. I decree that Your Spirit shall lift up a standard against every attack of the enemy.

As he meditates on Your Word day and night, cause him to be like a tree planted by rivers of living water that shall bring forth his fruit in his season.

I declare that he/she shall not be moved regardless of any present condition or circumstance.

I thank You Father that Your Word says, *"though the mountains depart and the hills be removed, yet your covenant of peace shall never be removed."*

I decree that Pastor _________________ will not allow his/her heart to be troubled, distressed, or agitated and his/her heart is fixed and trusted in Your daily.

In Jesus Name, Amen

Isaiah 26:3, "You will keep him in perfect peace whose mind is stayed on You because he trusts in You."

John 14:27, "Peace I leave with you, My peace I give to you; not as the world gives do I give to you. Let not your heart be troubled, neither let it be afraid."

Prayer for the Wisdom of God

Father, in the name of Jesus, I lift up my pastor unto You. Father, Your Word says that, *"Wisdom is the principal thing, and to exalt wisdom and she shall promote thee and she shall bring thee to honor."*

I pray that my pastor operates in the wisdom of God daily. Your Word declares that *"If anyone lacks wisdom let him ask of You who gives liberally to all men and upbraideth not."* May Your wisdom simplify anything that would ordinarily be difficult to grasp or ascertain.

I release Holy Spirit to cause the eyes of my pastor's understanding to be enlightened that he/she may be able to see around corners to navigate through seemingly difficult situations beyond the natural realm, to know things necessary by Your Spirit to cause supernatural results.

I thank You that as a result, projects and goals will be completed in an exceptional amount of time. Thank You Father for giving my pastor Your thoughts and Your heart and guiding him/her with the voice of Your wisdom daily.

In Jesus Name, Amen

Proverbs 4:4-8, "Get wisdom! Get understanding! Do not forget, nor turn away from the words of my mouth. Do not forsake her, and she will preserve you; love her and she will keep you. Wisdom is the principal thing; therefore get wisdom. And in all your getting, get understanding. Exalt her, and she will promote you; she will bring you honor, when you embrace her."

Proverbs 8:11, "For wisdom is better than rubies, and all the things one may desire cannot be compared with her."

The Favor of God

Father, in the name of Jesus, I thank You that my pastor is encompassed with the favor of God. For Your Word promises that You would encompass the righteous with favor as a shield. I decree that pastor's gift is bringing him before great men.

I thank You for opening doors before him/her that no man can close. Cause him/her to be preferred and sought out by the leaders of the land just as Daniel was because of the excellent spirit that was upon him.

Raise up people who will use their power, their ability, and their influence on his/her behalf to assist and support him/her in every endeavor. Allow Your favor to supersede above and beyond what money and education alone can do.

Cause Your goodness to be seen and greatly demonstrated in his/her life in order that men and women would be drawn unto You like never before. Your Word does declare that it is the goodness of the Lord that will cause men to repent.

I thank You that as men and women from all walks of life behold the favor and the goodness that You have displayed upon my pastor, that it will cause them to seek first Your kingdom and Your righteousness and to desire to know what must they do to be saved. Thank You, Father, that my pastor has abundant favor upon his/her life.

In Jesus Name, Amen

Psalms 5:12, "For You, O Lord, will bless the righteous; with favor You will surround him as with a shield."

Proverbs 8:33-35, "Hear instruction and be wise, and do not disdain it. Blessed is the man who listens to me, watching daily at my gates, waiting at the posts of my doors. For whoever finds me finds life and obtains favor from the Lord."

The Spirit of Excellence

Father, in the name of Jesus, I thank You that Pastor ________________ operates in an excellent spirit. I pray that excellence manifests in his/her character, family, relationships, ministry, assignments, and every decision.

I decree that whatever he/she does is done heartily as unto You and not unto men for their approval or applause.

I pray it is Pastor's desire always to maintain a good name, which You said, is better to be chosen than riches.

I decree that the excellence Pastor walks in causes him/her to be preferred and honored Justas, Your servant Daniel was.

I decree that many doors of opportunity are opened for the Word to go forth because of the diligent efforts that he/she always displays as he/she presents the gospel to the world.

As Pastor has set his/her heart to represent You in a first-class manner, may our local church arise like a city set on a hill that cannot be hidden because of the spirit of excellence that is here to meet the needs of Your people.

In Jesus Name, Amen

Colossians 3:23-24, "And whatever you do, do it heartily, as to the Lord and not to men, knowing that from the Lord you will receive the reward of the inheritance; for you serve the Lord Christ."

Proverbs 22:1, "A good name is to be chosen rather than great riches, loving favor rather than silver and gold."

Proverbs 22:29, "Do you see a man who excels in his work? He will stand before kings; He will not stand before unknown men."

Success of Ministry Conferences

Father, I lift our ministry conference to you. Thank you for birthing the desire in our pastors' heart to set aside this time to focus on a specific theme to further our growth and development in you!

I decree and declare that this will be a successful conference! I pray for every person that will be in attendance. I thank you that Holy Spirit is drawing men and women, boys and girls from every walk of life to attend this ministry conference. I pray that they will come seeking you like never before! I also pray that they are open to the leading and voice of Holy Spirit as he specifically speaks to them.

I bind every denominational barrier, spirits of tradition and religion from hindering the move of your spirit at this conference. I decree and declare that very yoke will be destroyed and every burden will be removed because of the anointing. I pray that there will be a faith fertile atmosphere that is charged with worship and praise!

Thank you father, for a word spoken in due season that will cause an internal and external change in the lives of your people. I pray that the result of this conference will be increase and promotion in the lives of your people.

In Jesus Name, Amen

---

1 Peter 4:8-11 "Above all, love each other deeply, because love covers over a multitude of sins. 9 Offer hospitality to one another without grumbling. 10 Each of you should use whatever gift you have received to serve others, as faithful stewards of God's grace in its various forms. 11 If anyone speaks, they should do so as one who speaks the very words of God. If anyone serves, they should do so with the strength God provides, so that in all things God may be praised through Jesus Christ. To him be the glory and the power for ever and ever. Amen."

Leader's and Assistants to Arise

Father, in the name of Jesus, I decree and declare that my pastor has good help to assist him in fulfilling the vision that you've given him. Your word shares that when Aaron and Hur upheld the arms of Moses, he continued to win the battle and as his arms grew heavy the army would persist against them. I, therefore, call forth the modern day Aaron's and Hurs to come and assist my Pastor.

I thank you for sending qualified people that have a true heart after you, and have received the heart of our Pastor to serve your people with a spirit of excellence. I pray that those who will assist him, will courageously take the helms of the different areas of ministry, taking ownership of it as if it were their very own.

I call forth those with the gifts of administration, creativity, teaching, organizing, psalmist and musicians and all needed areas of service to come to be a part of this God-given vision to assist our Pastor in the planning, growth, and development of your people. I pray that as a result of them giving their time, treasure and talent they will be blessed and our ministry will abundantly excel in service and edification of your people, like never before.

In Jesus Name, Amen

---

1 Corinthians 15:58 "Therefore, my beloved brothers, be steadfast, immovable, always abounding in the work of the Lord, knowing that in the Lord your labor is not in vain."

Jeremiah 3:15 "And I will give you shepherds after my own heart, who will feed you with knowledge and understanding."

The Rest of God

Father, we honor and praise Your great name! We thank you for Your word concerning entering into the rest of God. I pray that my Pastor keeps his mind fixed upon you, because your word promises that as he does, You will keep him in perfect peace. I pray that Pastor keeps Your word as first place in his life, each day by making it a priority to spend quality time reading and studying your word.

We ask You to continue to flood his heart and mind with the understanding of Your word like never before. Allow him to represent You in the earth as the mighty God, and loving Father that You are. I pray that his confident and vibrant relationship with You draws men and women to want to know You personally and passionately.

Thank You Lord, for always perfecting those things that concern him and showing Yourself as the faithful one who always keeps Your word. I declare that My pastor has entered into Your rest, and trusts you, with all of his/ her heart. I thank you Father for bringing to pass every dream, vision , and promise that You have given him/her. We love you Father, and we praise you for the amazing rest that only you can provide!

In Jesus Name, Amen

Isaiah 26:3 "You will keep him *in perfect peace,* Whose *mind* is *stayed* on You, *Because he trusts in You."*

Hebrews 4:9-11 "There remains therefore a rest for the people of God. 10 For he who has entered His rest has himself also ceased from his works as God did *from His."*

Matthew 6:33 33 But seek first the kingdom of God and His righteousness, and all these things shall be added to you."

Confession

I declare that my pastor is filled with the knowledge of Your will in all wisdom and spiritual understanding; that he/she walks worthy of You unto all pleasing and is fruitful in every good work, increasing in the knowledge of Your Word daily. As Pastor ________________ speaks Your Word, it will come forth in power and demonstration by Your Spirit and in much assurance.

I declare that Your Spirit rest upon him/her because You have anointed Pastor ______________ to preach good tidings unto the meek, to bind up the brokenhearted, to proclaim liberty to the captives, the opening of the prison to them that are bound, to proclaim the acceptable year of the Lord and the day of vengeance of our God

I decree that no weapon formed against him/her will prosper and every tongue that rises against him/her be condemned. Thank You that my pastor is a leader in the body of Christ that You have raised up for such a time as this to do great exploits in Your name, to cause many to see Your plan and purpose for their lives.

Thank You that You will fulfill all Your good pleasure through his/her life and ministry and with long life You will satisfy him/her and show him/her the blessing of salvation.

In Jesus Name, Amen

About the Author

Deborah Grant is the wife of Elder Donald Grant and the mother of three beautiful children, Jada, Donovan, and Nia. She was ordained in ministry in 1993 under the leadership of Dr's. Micheal and Dee Dee Freeman at the Spirit of Faith Christian Center.

She serves on the Pastoral Staff and is the Director of The Intercessory Prayer Ministry. She also serves as an instructor at the Spirit Of Faith Bible Institute, where she assist in the vision of her Pastor in training new ministerial leaders in fulfilling their calling and purpose. She is an accomplished author of now three books. Her second book entitled "Arise And Declare The Word!" speaks to the believer's responsibility to speak with their God-ordained authority and faith concerning situations and circumstances that they will face in life. Her third and latest book entitled, “Powerful People Praying Together”, empowers and equips the people of God to discover the power of agreement in prayer.

She is a powerful teacher of the word of God! Her heart’s desire is to see people empowered through the word and to achieve their full potential in life! Minister Grant is also a skilled prayer warrior and has served as the lead Intercessor at Spirit of Faith Christian Center for over 20 years! In 2016 she started and began hosting a weekly prayer conference call, along with a team of intercessors on behalf of the SOFCC Ministry. She is a requested conference speaker that delivers the word with practical application lessons every time! You will be blessed, as you encounter and receive her ministry!